Dear Parents,

Children's earliest experiences with stories and books usually involve grown-ups reading to them. However, reading should be active, and as adults, we can help young readers make meaning of the text by prompting them to relate the book to what they already know and to their personal experiences. Our questions will lead them to move beyond the simple story and pictures and encourage them to think beneath the surface. For example, after reading a story about the sleep habits of animals, you might ask, "Do you remember when you moved into a big bed? Could you see the moon out of your window?"

Illustrations in these books are wonderful and can be used in a variety of ways. Your questions about them can direct the child to details and encourage him or her to think about what those details tell us about the story. You might ask the child to find three different "beds" used by animals and insects in the book. Illustrations can even be used to inspire readers to draw their own pictures related to the text.

At the end of each book, there are some suggested questions and activities related to the story. These questions range in difficulty and will help you move young readers from the text itself to thinking skills such as comparing and contrasting, predicting, applying what they learned to new situations and identifying things they want to find out more about. This conversation about their reading may even result in the children becoming the storytellers, rather than simply the listeners!

Harriet Ziefert, M.A.
Language Arts/Reading Specialist

More to  About

Does a Bear Wear Boots?

Does a Beaver Sleep in a Bed?

Does a Camel Cook Spaghetti?

Does a Hippo Go to the Doctor?

Does an Owl Wear Eyeglasses?

Does a Panda Go to School?

Does a Tiger Go to the Dentist?

Does a Woodpecker Use a Hammer?

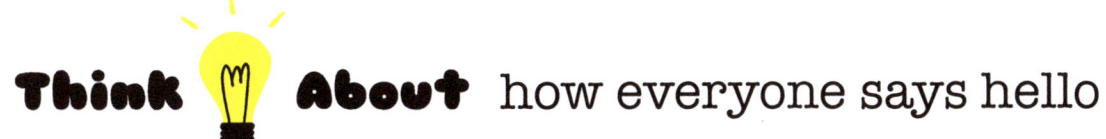 how everyone says hello

Does a Seal Smile?

Harriet Ziefert • illustrations by **Emily Bolam**

BLUE APPLE

Text copyright © 2006, 2014 by Harriet Ziefert
Illustrations copyright © 2006 by Emily Bolam
All rights reserved
CIP data is available.
Published in the United States 2014 by
Blue Apple Books
South Orange, New Jersey
www.blueapplebooks.com

Does a seal smile?

Does a mandrill smile?

A mandrill does not smile.
This mandrill's expression is really more snarl than smile.

He is opening his mouth and showing his teeth to show he is angry.

Does a coyote smile?

A coyote does not smile.

Coyotes use facial expressions to communicate, but they do not smile.

Does a chimp smile?

A chimp *almost* smiles.
Chimpanzees are social animals.

They can make many
different facial expressions
and sounds to go along with them.

Chimps greet other chimps in different ways.
A person who knows chimps learns what the
chimp means by the position of the tail,
the arms, the legs—the chimp's whole body.

What do you think these chimps are communicating?

But no animal has as many ways of greeting another member of its species as a human being.

When a baby is six weeks old, it smiles when it sees another person.

At six months old, a baby smiles, waves his arms, and kicks his legs when he sees a familiar face. The baby shows excitement and happiness.

At around nine months,
a baby sometimes shows
that she doesn't know a person
by using an unfriendly expression.

A year-old baby can wave bye-bye.

Soon after, the baby will speak and say, "Hi!"

Small children give hugs and kisses when they greet people they know.

And when they see people they don't know,
they sometimes hide their faces.

People use many more ways to greet one another than animals. They use lots of different expressions.

Nice to meet you!

Buenos días!

Bonjour!

Ciao!

They can shake hands,

 slap a high five,

and hug each other.

People greet each other differently.

In Korea, they bow slightly and shake hands.

In Japan, they bow to each other.

In France, they kiss once on each cheek.

In Greece, they wave "hello."

Men and women greet each other differently.

Pakistan

Egypt

India

Saudi Arabia

How do you greet someone you know?

Think  About how everyone says hello

This book compares the greeting behaviors of a seal, a mandrill, a coyote, and a chimp to the ways that people greet one another.

Compare and Contrast

- How do two cats greet each other?
  How does a cat greet a person?
- How do two dogs greet each other?
  How does a dog greet a person?

Compare how people greet one another in other countries.

- Act each out with a friend. Which do you like best?

Research

Go to a library or online and find out:

- How does a peacock greet another peacock?
- How does a polar bear greet another polar bear?
- How does a baboon greet another baboon?

Look online, in the library, or ask people you know, how to say "hello" in another language.

- Teach someone else what you learn.

Observe

Watch a baby for 15 minutes.

- What greeting behaviors do you see?

(speaking, waving, hugging, kissing, smiling, making noises, body movements….)

How does each member of your family (people and pets) greet you in the morning?

- Make a list and think about why they are different.

At pick-up time at school, watch how kids greet their parents or caregivers.

- What is the most common thing they say when they meet?

Write, Tell, or Draw

Write a story about "hello" or "goodbye."

Create a story where everyone in your classroom is a dog or another animal. You have not seen one another for a long time.

- How do you act? What happens?

Make up a new way to greet a friend.

- Draw an instruction sheet for your friend so she or he can start greeting you that way, too.

www.ingramcontent.com/pod-product-compliance
Lightning Source LLC
LaVergne TN
LVHW070837080426
835510LV00026B/3426